Contents

Answers are on the back of the Pull-out Poster in the centre of the book.

This book covers unit 3F from the year three scheme of work

Published by Coordination Group Publications Ltd.

Contributors:
Taissa Csáky
Chris Dennett
Dominic Hall
Tim Major
Becky May
Katherine Reed
Claire Thompson
James Paul Wallis

ISBN: 978 1 84146 251 6

Groovy website: www.cgpbooks.co.uk
Jolly bits of clipart from CorelDRAW®
Printed by Elanders Hindson Ltd, Newcastle upon Tyne.

With thanks to Christine Tinkler and Glenn Rogers for the proofreading.

Background — Light and Dark

During the day it's light, and at night it's dark.

Q1   Use the words in the black box to label the things in these two pictures.
Then use the words in the grey box to finish the sentences.

| SUN   LAMP   SHADOW   EARTH |

| NIGHT   LIGHT   DAY   DARK |

....

....

In this picture it is .... time. It's .... outside.

....

....

In this picture it is .... -time. It's .... outside.

Q2   Finish the sentences below. Ring the correct words in the brackets.

The (SHADOW / SUN) is the main source of light in the daytime picture.

The (LAMP / DOG BOWL) is the main source of light in the night-time picture.

Sunshine makes light — how de-light-ful...

Most of our light comes from the Sun during the day. When the Sun sets there's no more sunshine. That's why it's dark at night. Remember that we need light to see things.

Torch Shadows

Light can come from light bulbs, torches and lamps.
But where does it go?

Q1 Draw a **straight arrow** to show where the light goes in each picture.
The first one has been done for you.

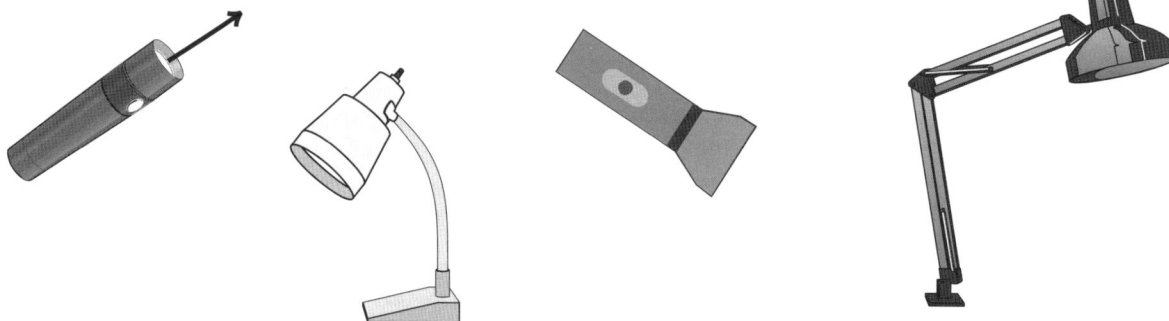

Q2 Choose words from the torch to complete the sentences.

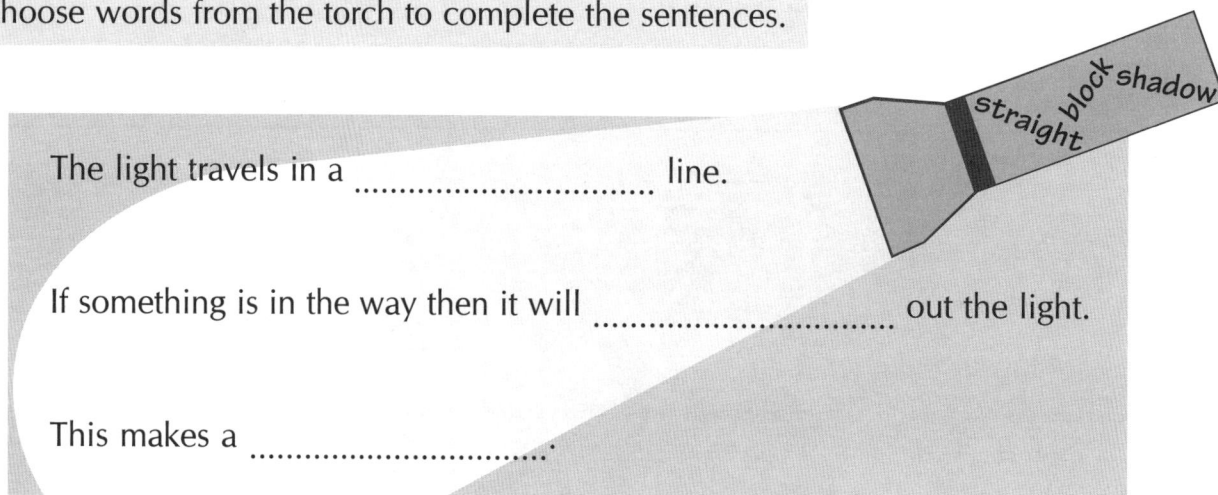

straight block shadow

The light travels in a .... line.

If something is in the way then it will .... out the light.

This makes a ....

Q3 There is only a shadow if an object blocks the light.
Tick (✓) the picture below where there will be a shadow.

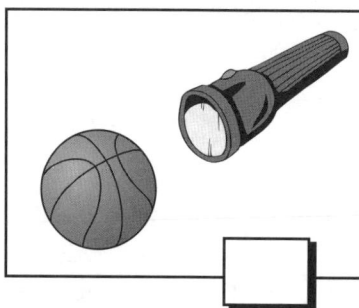

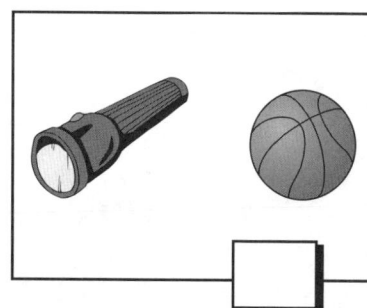

Did you hear about the man hit with a torch?...

If you are trying this out, make sure you have a good strong torch with a bright light.
If not, you won't be able to see the shadows properly.

Torch Shadows

Shadows are a lot more fun than you might think —
they come in all shapes and sizes...

© CGP 2003

Q1 Choose the correct words to describe the
shadows of these different objects.

round long, thin triangular

A football has a .... shadow.

A pencil has a .... shadow.

A pyramid has a .... shadow.

Q2 Look at the picture below and tick (✓) the correct shadow.

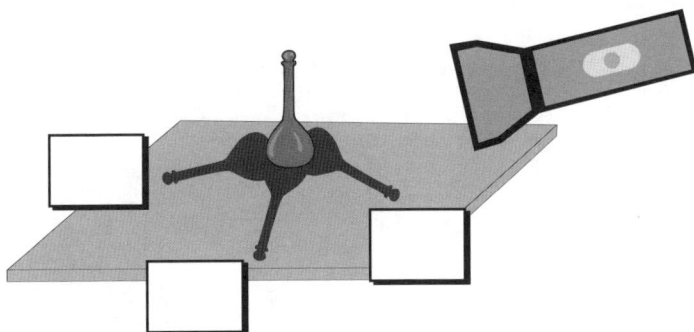

There was something funny
about Tim's shadow.

Q3 In the pictures below the shadows are missing. Complete the
pictures by drawing the shadow. I've done the first one for you.

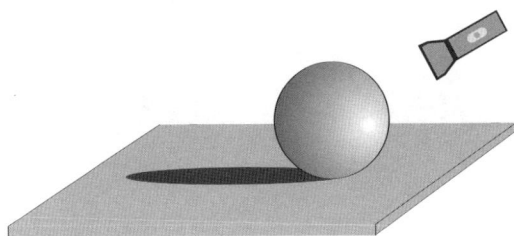

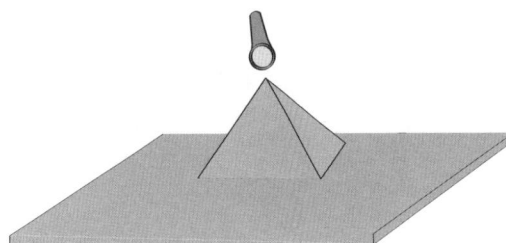

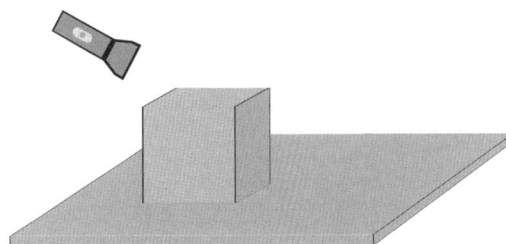

...He was a shadow of his former self...

There are only two things you really need to remember — light travels in a straight line,
and when something blocks the light you get a shadow. Simple as that.

Sun Shadows

The Sun is a like a massive torch in the sky. When the light is blocked,
you get a shadow — same as you do with a torch.

Q1 Draw a line from each person to their shadow.

Q2 When the Sun is very hot we can stay in the shade to keep cool and avoid sunburn.
Draw a cross (✖) on each picture to show where you should stand to be in the shade.

The Sun has got his hat on...

Be careful. The Sun is **VERY** bright and it's really bad for your eyes if you look straight
at it — you could even go blind. So don't look straight at the Sun...

Sun Shadows

The Sun is great, because it makes BIG shadows. Check these out...

Q1 Complete this picture by drawing in the shadows. I've done the tree for you.

Q2 Charley draws a chalk outline around the shadow of a lamp-post in the morning. Circle the correct words to complete these sentences about the shadow.

If Charley checks the shadow in the afternoon it will be in [the same / a different] place.

The shadow is made when [a cloud / the lamp-post] blocks light from the [Sun / ground].

The [lamp-post / Sun] moves during the day, so the [lamp-post / shadow] moves too.

...casting a massive shadow over Preston...

The Sun can cast huge shadows — from trees, houses, double-decker buses... What's even cooler is that as the Sun moves so do the shadows. Now that's cool.

© CGP 2003

6

Do Shadows Change?

This is a massive four-page experiment to find out
how shadows change during the day.

Q1   Tick (✓) three things you could test about shadows.

length   good at   darkness   joke-telling   direction
                games

It's best to test __one thing__ at a time when you do an
experiment. This experiment tests how the __lengths__
of shadows change during the day.

You need to set up a __stick__ in the
playground. You will measure the length
of the stick's __shadow__ during the day.

Q2   Tick (✓) the three things you should do for the experiment to work and be a fair test.

☐   Do the experiment on a cloudy day so there isn't much light.

☐   Measure the shadow of the stick several times during the day.

☐   Only measure the shadow of the stick at 11 o'clock.

☐   Measure the shadow of the same stick each time.

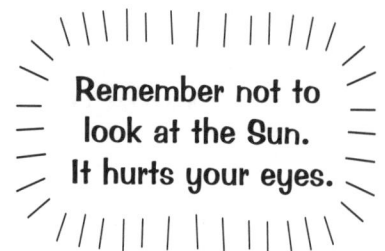

Remember not to
look at the Sun.
It hurts your eyes.

☐   Measure the shadow of a different stick each time.

☐   Do the experiment on a sunny day so you can see a strong shadow.

Light and Stick — a couple of shady characters...

Sorry to keep going on about fair tests. Just make sure it's only the thing you are testing
that changes during the experiment — otherwise your results will be screwy.

Do Shadows Change?

It's good to work out what you're going to do before you start
— that way you're less likely to get in a muddle.

Q1 The picture shows the experiment. Use words from the splodge to fill in the labels.

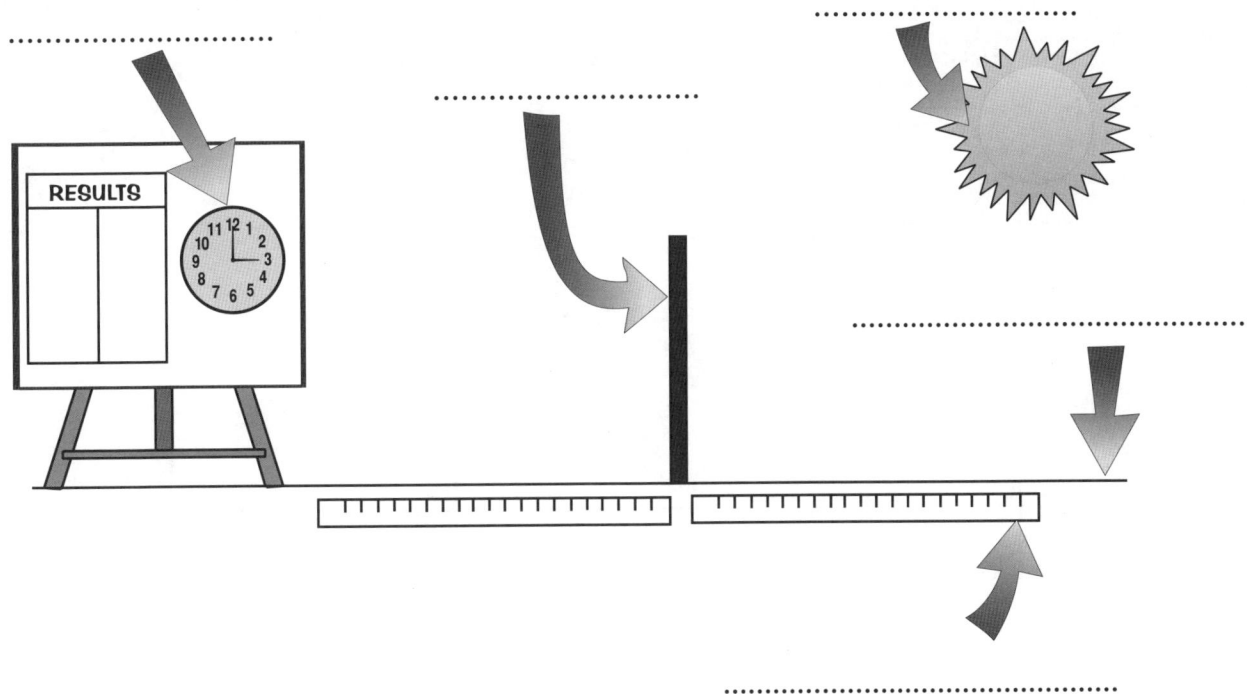

RESULTS

TAPE MEASURE   STICK   CLOCK   THE SUN   FLAT GROUND

Q2 Write **1**, **2**, **3** and **4** next to the sentences to show what order you should do things in.

.... Measure from the base of the stick to the chalk mark with a tape measure.

.... Set up a stick in the playground and look at its shadow at five different times during the day.

.... Use chalk to mark the length of the shadow.

.... Finally, write the measurements into a results table.

No lights in the theatre — shadow play...

So you've worked out what you're doing. Now it's time to do the experiment.
I've drawn out a table on the next page for you to write your results in. Good luck.

8

Do Shadows Change?

When you first get your results they can be a confusing muddle —
putting them into a table or bar chart makes it easier to see a pattern.

Q1   Write your results in the table.

If you didn't do the experiment you can use my spare results at the bottom of the page.

TIME OF DAY	9 am	10:30 am	12 noon	1:30 pm	3 pm
LENGTH OF SHADOW (cm)					

Q2   Now use the results to fill in the bar chart.

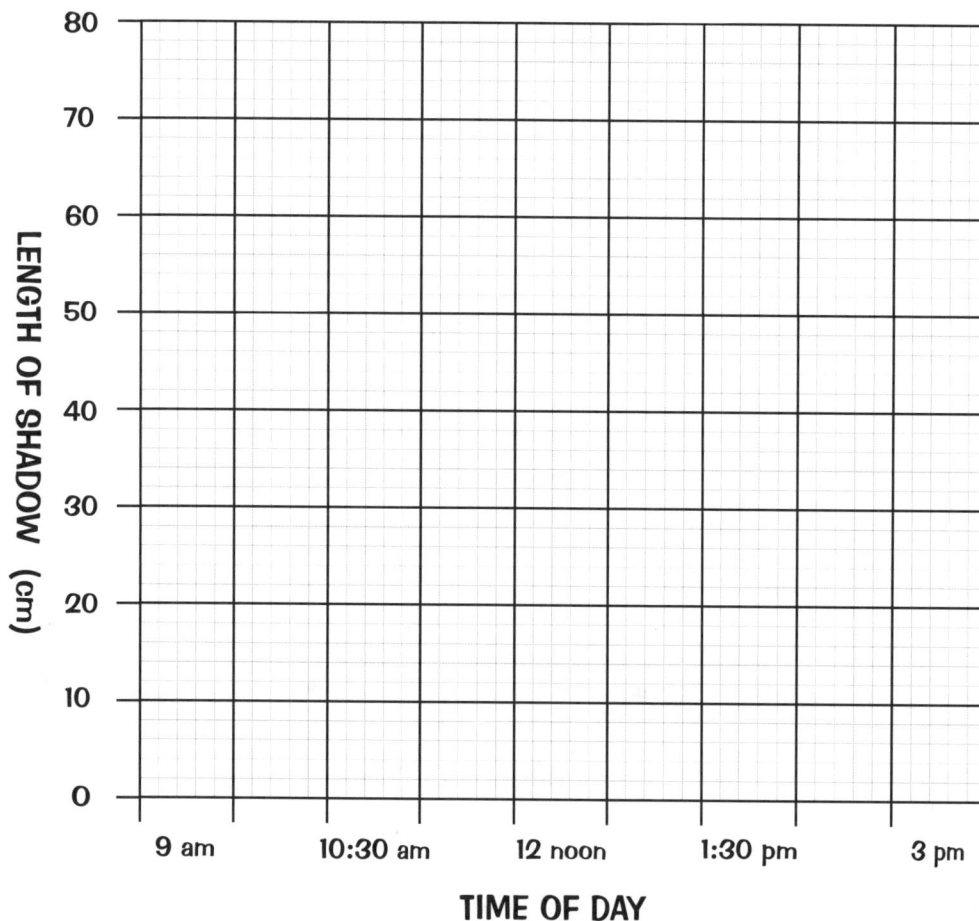

Bar charts look like this.

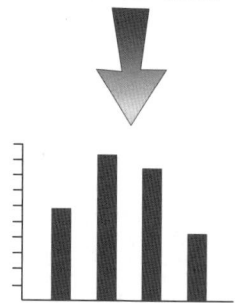

LENGTH OF SHADOW (cm) — 0, 10, 20, 30, 40, 50, 60, 70, 80

TIME OF DAY: 9 am, 10:30 am, 12 noon, 1:30 pm, 3 pm

Singing sheep — the baa chart...

The bar chart is the tricky bit — ask your teacher or some passing busybody for help.
Don't go onto the next page without doing the bar chart — it helps with the next question.

© CGP 2003

Do Shadows Change?

MINI-PROJECT

You've got the experiment all wrapped up.
But don't go home and watch TV just yet — work out a conclusion first.

Q1 (Circle) the right words for the conclusion to make sense.

The stick had a shadow because it BLOCKED OUT / LET THROUGH light from the Sun.

The length of the stick's shadow CHANGED / STAYED THE SAME during the day.

Until 12 noon the shadow got LONGER / SHORTER.

After 12 noon the shadow got LONGER / SHORTER.

The shadow was LONGEST / SHORTEST at 12 noon.

Reg didn't want to see the words LONG and SHORT ever again.

Q2 Draw a shadow and arrow on the pictures for **10 am** and **3 pm**. Work out how long the shadow should be by looking at the length of the shadows at other times of day.

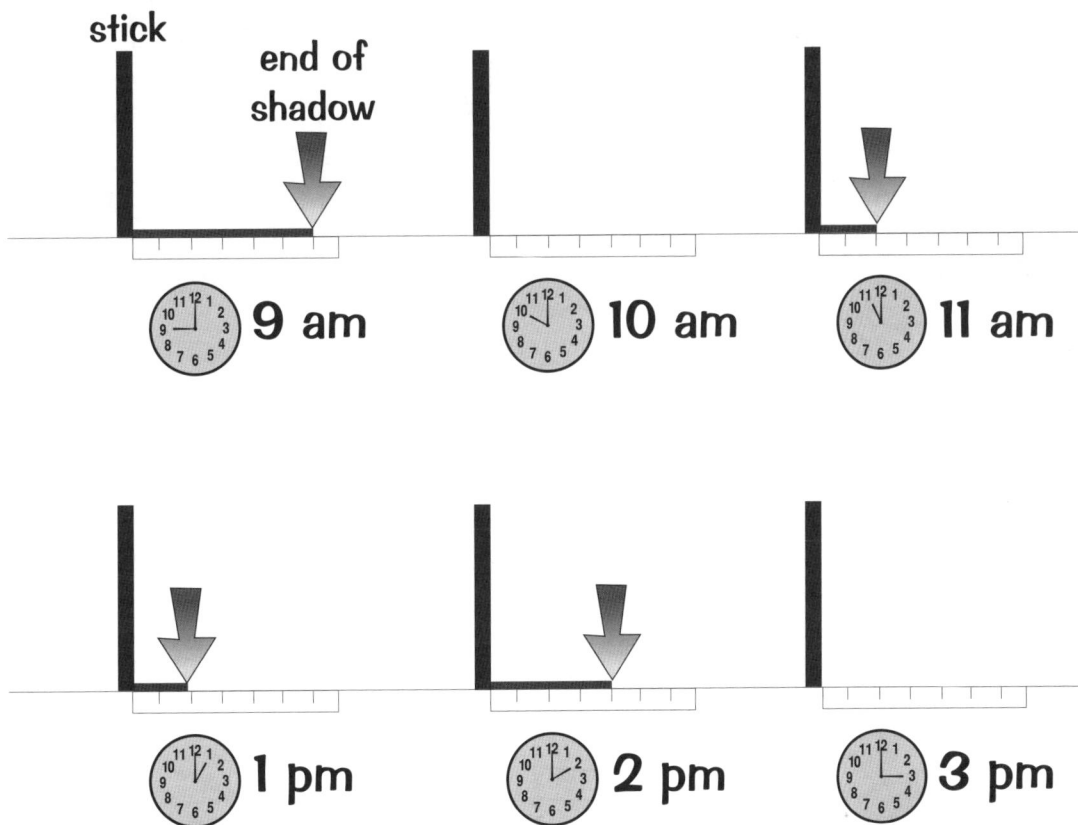

stick — end of shadow

9 am **10 am** **11 am**

1 pm **2 pm** **3 pm**

Engine failure — the mini-project's downfall...

In four pages you've worked out how the lengths of shadows change during the day.
Time to swing back in your chair and reward yourself with chocolate.

The Sun Does the Same Thing Every Day

During the day the Sun seems to move across the sky.
It rises in one place and sets in another.

Q1 It's a sunny day at school. Look at each picture — notice the time and which window the Sun is shining through. Answer the question with YES or NO.

1) 10:00 am

2) 1:00 pm

3) 4:00 pm

Does the Sun seem to be moving through the sky? ....

Q2 The Sun does the same thing every day. The picture below shows the same classroom **at 1 pm** the next day. Draw the Sun in the correct window.

1:00 pm

Q3 Tick the box next to the correct picture of the Sun's path through the sky.

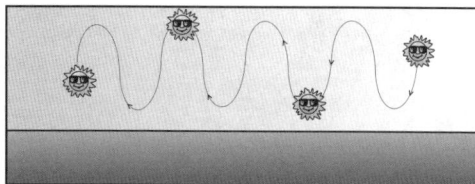

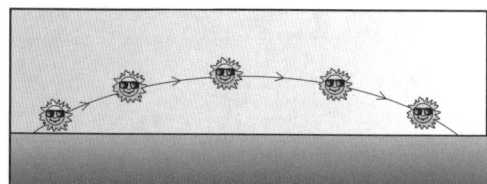

A smart Sun — always in its Sun-day best...

The Sun must have a boring life — it does the <u>same</u> thing every day. Think about when the Sun shines through different windows in your classroom. It's always the same.

More About Sun Shadows

When something blocks sunlight a shadow is made.

Q1   Put a tick in the box next to the correct picture of the Sun making a shadow.

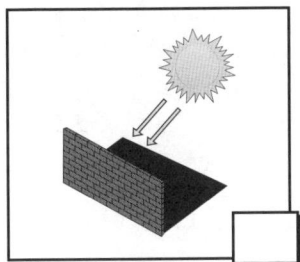

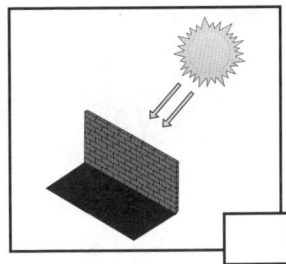

Q2   Write TRUE or FALSE for each of the sentences below.

1)   My shadow is **in front of me** when I face the Sun.

....

2)   My shadow is **behind me** when I face the Sun.

....

Rodney wished his
shadow would keep
up with him.

Q3   The pictures show Deidre and her shadow. For each picture draw the Sun and
an arrow showing the direction of the sunlight. I've done the first one for you.

No shadow of a doubt — the Sun's bright...

Remember that shadows are made when something blocks sunlight. Shadows are always
on the opposite side of things to the Sun — as though they're trying to hide from the Sun.

8

Sun Shadows Move

The Sun's position in the sky changes during the day.
That makes all the shadows move too.

A class set up a shadow stick in the playground. They drew round the shadow it made on the ground at different times of the day.

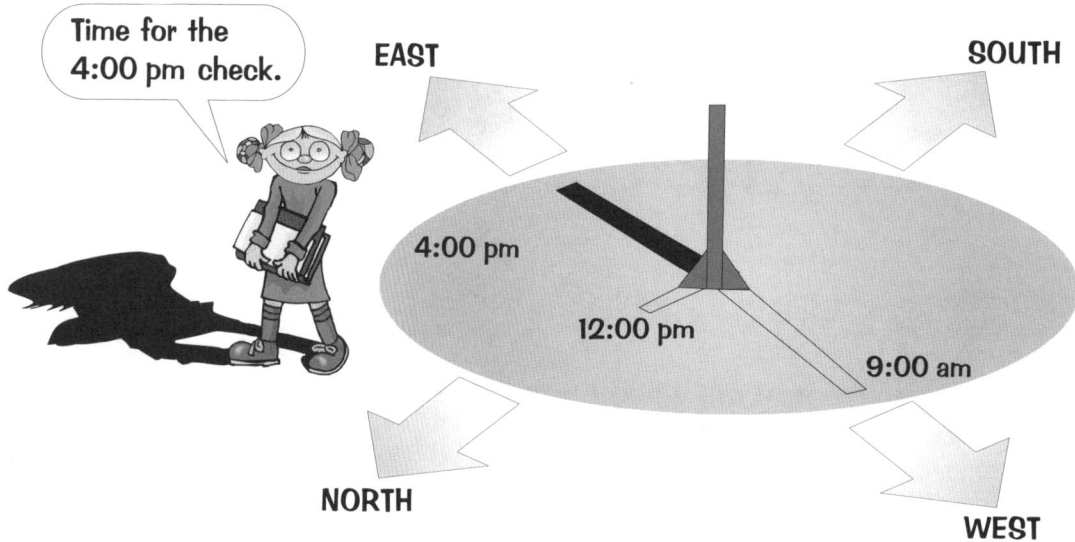

Time for the 4:00 pm check.

EAST

SOUTH

4:00 pm

12:00 pm

9:00 am

NORTH

WEST

Q1 Next to each time, write which way the shadow was pointing. I've done the first one for you.

9 am .....*WEST*.....

12 pm ....

4 pm ....

Maurice spent many happy days trying to jump over his shadow.

Q2 Now write where the Sun was at different times. I've helped you with the first one.

9 am *in the EAST* .... 12 pm .... 4 pm ....

The class did the same thing for three days. The shadows were the same every day.

The Sun follows the SAME path through the sky EVERY DAY.

Don't mess with the Sun — you'll get a shiner...

Shadows are always on the opposite side of things to the Sun. As the Sun changes position in the sky the shadows move too. Clever things these shadows.

© CGP 2003

KS2 Science Answers — Light and Shadows

Page 15 The Spinning Earth

Q1: a) It is **NIGHT-TIME** in India. b) It is **DAYTIME** in Australia.

c) It is **NIGHT-TIME** in S. Africa. d) It is **DAYTIME** in Canada.

Page 16 Sundials

Q1:

The stick part is called the GNOMON

The shadow says it is about 3 o'clock

A simple shadow clock — just a stick in the ground.

Ancient Egyptians had big stone pillars.

Q2: Give a mark for any relevant, factually accurate information.

Page 17 Problems with Sundials

Q1: a) It's night-time, so there's no shadow.
b) It's cloudy, so there's no shadow.
c) The sundial is in the shade, so there's no shadow.
d) The sundial is indoors, so there's no shadow.
e) The sundial is facing the wrong way, so it's telling the wrong time.

Page 18 Mini-Project — Shadows of Different Materials

Q1: Lets lots of light through | Lets some light through | Lets no light through

Q2: These materials are **opaque**. They let **NO** light through.
Opaque items let **NO** light through.
These materials are **transparent**.
They let **LOTS OF** light through.
Transparent items let **LOTS OF** light through.
These materials are **translucent**.
They let **SOME** light through.
Translucent items let **SOME** light through.

Page 19 Mini-Project — Shadows of Different Materials

Q1:
TRANSLUCENT OBJECTS
HINT: Remember these let SOME light through.

OPAQUE OBJECTS
HINT: Remember these let NO light through.

TRANSPARENT OBJECTS
HINT: Remember these let LOTS OF light through.

Pale, faint shadow | Not very dark shadow | Very dark shadow

Q2:

Objects	They block out	The shadow will be
Opaque	all the light	dark, black
Transparent	hardly any light	pale, faint
Translucent	some light	not very dark

Page 20 Mini-Project — Shadows of Different Materials

Q1:

puny, dull torch

big, strong torch

a big cake

collection of translucent, transparent and opaque things

white paper or cardboard to look at the shadow on

Q2: The correct choices are:
1. Get 1 opaque, 1 transparent and 1 translucent material.
2. Hold the objects over a piece of white cardboard.
3. Shine the same torch on each of the samples.
4. Sketch and write down what the shadows look like.

Page 21 Mini-Project — Shadows of Different Materials

Q1: Opaque: The shadow is **VERY DARK**.
Transparent: The shadow is **PALE AND FAINT**.
Translucent: The shadow is **NOT VERY DARK**.

Q2: OPAQUE   TRANSLUCENT   TRANSPARENT

Page 22 Mini-Project, Shadows of Different Materials

Q1:

Objects	They blocked out	The shadow was
Opaque	all the light	very dark
Transparent	hardly any light	pale, faint
Translucent	some light	not very dark

Q2: Shadows are made when an object blocks **LIGHT**.
Opaque, transparent and translucent objects block **DIFFERENT** amounts of light.
This means that their **SHADOWS** look different.
The more light an object blocks out, the **DARKER** its shadow will be.

Page 23 Revision Questions

Q1: The Sun

Q2: Shadows are made when objects **BLOCK** light.
The **FIRST** picture should be ticked.

Q3:

Q4:

Page 24 Revision Questions

Q5: a) FALSE
b) TRUE

Q6: The **SECOND** picture should be ticked.

Q7: The Sun does **THE SAME THING** every day.

Q8:

Q9: a) ②
b) **HIGH**

Page 25 Revision Questions

Q10: The Earth **SPINS** round once each day.
This makes the **SUN** seem to move through the sky.
But the Sun actually stays **STILL**.

Q11: Any two of these: When it's cloudy / night-time / indoors / in the shade / or the sundial is facing the wrong way.

Q12:

TYPE OF MATERIAL	AMOUNT OF LIGHT LET THROUGH	EXAMPLE
OPAQUE	Lets no light through	Wood/brick etc.
TRANSLUCENT	Lets some light through	Nylon tights
TRANSPARENT	Lets lots of light through	Milk bottle

Q13: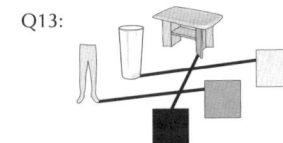

LIGHT and SHADOWs

The shadow on a sundial can be used to tell the time.

Glass
transpa

The Sun is low in the sky.

The Sun is high in the sky.

Long shadows

Short shadows

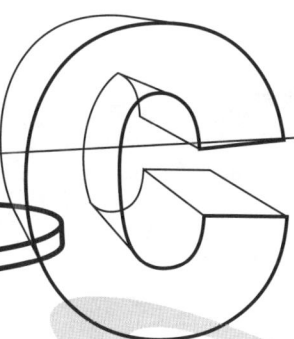

Jelly is <u>translucent</u>.

Stone is <u>opaque</u>.

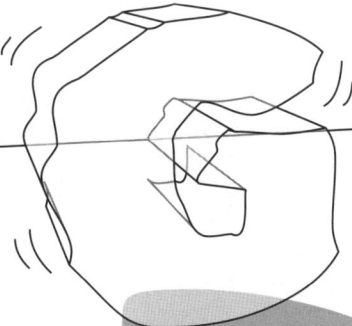

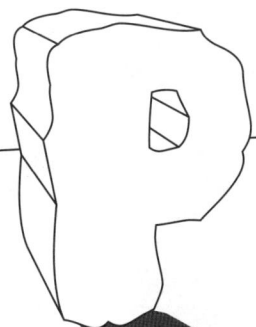

Dark shadow

nt.

Very faint shadow

Quite faint shadow

KS2 Science Answers — Light and Shadows

Page 1 Background — Light and Dark

Q1:

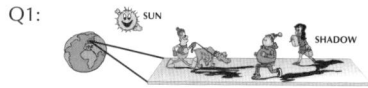

In this picture it is **DAY**time. It's **LIGHT** outside.

In this picture it is **NIGHT**-time. It's **DARK** outside.

Q2: The **SUN** is the main source of light in the daytime picture.
The **LAMP** is the main source of light in the night-time picture.

Page 2 Torch Shadows

Q1:

Q2: The light travels in a **STRAIGHT** line.
If something is in the way then it will **BLOCK** out the light.
This makes a **SHADOW**.

Q3: The **MIDDLE** picture should be ticked.

Page 3 Torch Shadows

Q1: A football has a **ROUND** shadow.
A pencil has a **LONG, THIN** shadow.
A pyramid has a **TRIANGULAR** shadow.

Q2:

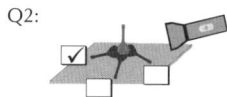

Q3:

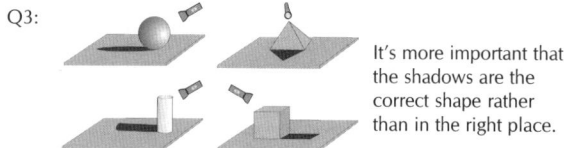

It's more important that the shadows are the correct shape rather than in the right place.

Page 4 Sun Shadows

Q1:

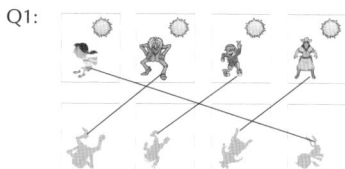

Q2:

Page 5 Sun Shadows

Q1:

Q2: If Charley checks the shadow in the afternoon it will be in **A DIFFERENT** place.
The shadow is made when **THE LAMP-POST** blocks light from the **SUN**.
The **SUN** moves during the day, so the **SHADOW** moves too.

Page 6 Mini-Project — Do Shadows Change?

Q1: **LENGTH, DARKNESS** and **DIRECTION** should be ticked.
Q2: Measure the shadow of the stick several times during the day.
Measure the shadow of the same stick each time.
Do the experiment on a sunny day so you can see a strong shadow.

Page 7 Mini-Project — Do Shadows Change?

Q1:

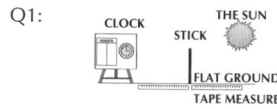

Q2: 3 Measure from the base of the stick...
1 Set up a stick in the playground ...
2 Use chalk to mark the length of the shadow.
4 Finally, write the measurements in a results table.

Page 8 Mini-Project — Do Shadows Change?

The answers will depend on your results. Using the spare results:

Q1:

TIME OF DAY	9 am	10:30 am	12 noon	1:30 pm	3 pm
LENGTH OF SHADOW	70	40	15	40	70

Q2:

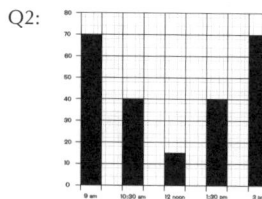

Page 9 Mini-Project — Do Shadows Change?

Q1: The stick had a shadow because it **BLOCKED OUT** light from the Sun.
The length of the stick's shadow **CHANGED** during the day.
Until 12 noon the shadow got **SHORTER**.
After 12 noon the shadow got **LONGER**.
The shadow was **SHORTEST** at 12 noon.

Q2:

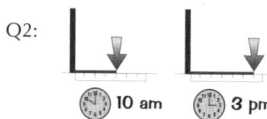

Page 10 The Sun Does the Same Thing Every Day

Q1: Yes
Q2:

Q3: The **SECOND** picture should be ticked.

Page 11 More About Sun Shadows

Q1: The **SECOND** picture should be ticked.
Q2: 1) FALSE   2) TRUE
Q3:

Page 12 Sun Shadows Move

Q1: 12 pm **NORTH**; 4 pm **EAST**
Q2: 12 pm **in the SOUTH**; 4 pm **in the WEST**

Page 13 Sun Shadows Change Length

Q1: When was the shadow shortest? **MIDDAY**
When was the shadow longest? **MORNING** and **AFTERNOON**
Q2: The shadow was shortest at **12 pm**.
That means the Sun was **HIGHEST** at that time.
At 9 am and 4 pm the shadow was **LONG**.
The Sun was **LOW** at those times.

Page 14 The Spinning Earth

Q1:

Q2: The Earth is **SPINNING**. It spins round once every day. The Sun **STAYS** where it is, while the **EARTH** spins. We can only **SEE** the Sun when our side of the Earth is facing the right way. It's **DAYTIME** when we're facing the Sun and it's night-time when we're facing **AWAY** from the Sun.

Sun Shadows Change Length

The Sun seems to change height in the sky during the day. When the Sun looks higher shadows are short. When the Sun looks lower in the sky shadows are long.

Q1 Look at the shadow stick picture on page 12 again.
Use the words in the Sun to answer the questions.

morning
afternoon
midday

When was the shadow shortest?

....

When was the shadow longest? Give two times.

.... and ....

Q2 Put a (ring) round the correct words in brackets to finish these sentences.
Use the pictures of the torch to help you.

The shadow was shortest at (9 am / 12 pm).

That means the Sun was (HIGHEST / LOWEST) at that time.

**The torch is high.
The shadow is short.**

At 9 am and 4 pm the shadow was (LONG / SHORT).

The Sun was (HIGH / LOW) at those times.

**The torch is low.
The shadow is long.**

Sun days are better than others...

When the Sun rises it's low in the sky. It rises until midday. Then it starts to get lower again, until it finally sets. Kind of like this...

The Spinning Earth

Everyone knows the Sun rises every morning and sets every night
— it looks as if the Sun is moving round the Earth.

But it's really the <u>Earth</u> that's <u>spinning</u> — which makes it *look* as if the Sun's moving.

Q1 Label the EARTH and the SUN in this picture.

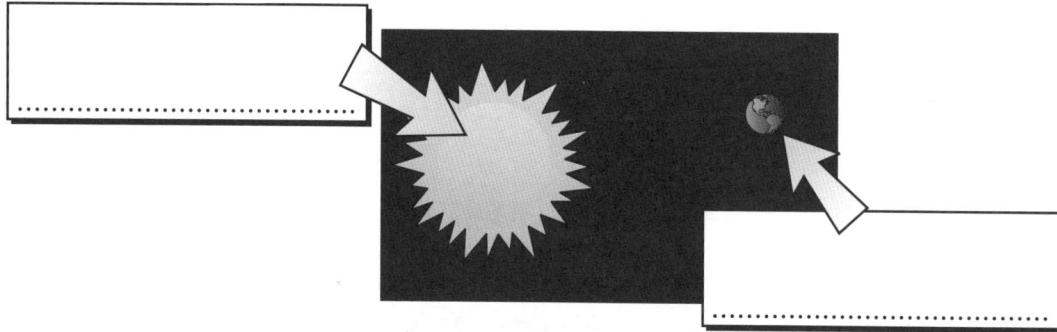

....

....

Q2 Fill in the gaps to explain how the Earth moves. Pick the right words from the splodge.

The Earth is .... It spins round once every day.

The Sun .... where it is, while the .... spins.

spinning away dangerous Sun see stays Earth towards daytime

We can only .... the Sun when our side of the Earth is facing the right way.

It's .... when we're facing the Sun

and it's night-time when we're facing .... from the Sun.

PLAYGROUND GAME:

*Stick the word "SUN" on your mate's forehead.
Stick the word "EARTH" on your head.
Spin round like mad.
It looks as though your friend is walking round you.
But it's you that's moving.
That's a bit like the Earth and Sun.
(Except the Earth doesn't get dizzy.)*

The Sun has got his hat on...

Confusing, huh. The Earth spins round — once a day. The Sun stays put.
We can only see the Sun when our side of the Earth is facing the right way.

The Spinning Earth

When it's daytime here, it's night-time in Australia.
That's because Australia's on the other side of the world from us.
When Britain is facing the Sun, the other half of the world is in shadow.

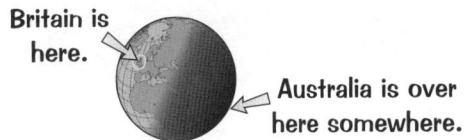

Britain is here.

Australia is over here somewhere.

Q1 Draw and colour the shadow onto each picture of the Earth.
Then say if it's DAYTIME or NIGHT-TIME in the country labelled.

a) SUN

India

It is .... in India.

b) SUN

Australia

It is .... in Australia.

c) SUN

South Africa

It is .... in South Africa.

d) SUN

Canada

It is .... in Canada.

...but he's not going anywhere...*

It's _daytime_ in Britain when Britain is _facing the Sun_. When Britain is _facing away_ from the Sun, Britain is in _shadow_. Which means it's night-time and you're tucked up in bed.

* Doesn't have quite the same ring somehow...

<u>Sundials</u>

Shadows change during the day, so you can use them to tell the time.
People have used shadow clocks for thousands of years.

Q1   Some of the labels are missing on these pictures.
      Choose the right labels from the box — then write them in the spaces.

The shadow says it is about three o'clock.

The stick part is called the GNOMON.

Ancient Egyptians had big stone pillars.

A simple shadow clock — just a stick in the ground.

....

....

....

The lines on a sundial are to mark the hours.

....

....

....

A sundial has to face the right way — or it won't tell the time properly.

....

....

....

....

....

....

....

People could tell the time from far away.

Q2   Find a book or a website about sundials and shadow clocks.
      Write down **one** thing about them that **isn't** in Question 1.

....

....

<u>What's the time Mr Wolf...</u> Sun

The Egyptians were building their pillars in 3500 BC — that's 5500 years ago!

Problems with Sundials

Normal clocks work any time, anywhere — but sundials only work in the sunshine.

Q1   Frank has problems with his sundial.
For each picture, write down why Frank **can't** tell the time.

a)

....

....

....

b)

....

....

....

c)

....

....

....

d)

....

....

....

e)

....

....

....

Sundials — they can be tricky...

Sundials are so simple you could make one yourself. But they won't work unless it's sunny.

MINI-PROJECT

Shadows of Different Materials

Different materials let different amounts of light through...

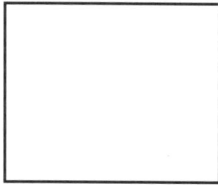

Q1 Draw a picture of each thing in the right box.

> glass window   blindfold   sunglasses   nylon tights

Lets lots of light through	Let some light through		Lets no light through

Q2 Write LOTS OF, SOME or NO to complete the sentences.

OPAQUE

These materials are **opaque**.

They let .... light through.

Opaque items let .... light through.

TRANSPARENT

These materials are **transparent**.

They let .... light through.

Transparent items let .... light through.

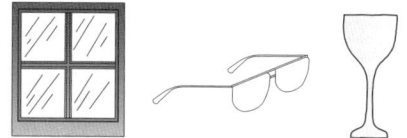

TRANSLUCENT

plastic carrier bag

nylon tights   tracing paper

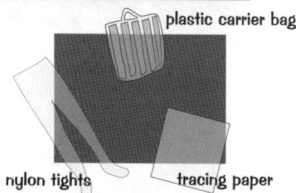

These materials are **translucent**.

They let .... light through.

Translucent items let .... light through.

Transparent as mud?...

Opaque, transparent and translucent are tricky words just to describe how much light things let through — but you need to remember them or this experiment will get very confusing.

Shadows of Different Materials

If materials let different amounts of light through,
they might have different types of shadows...

Q1 Draw a line to match each type of object to
the type of shadow you think it will have.

TRANSLUCENT OBJECTS

HINT: Remember these let SOME light through.

OPAQUE OBJECTS

HINT: Remember these let NO light through.

TRANSPARENT OBJECTS

HINT: Remember these let LOTS OF light through.

Pale, faint shadow   Not very dark shadow   Very dark shadow

Highlights Night Club

No light was allowed through.

Q2 Fill in this prediction table to say what type
of shadow you think each material will have.

Objects	They block out	The shadow will be
Opaque	all the light	dark, black
Transparent	....	....
Translucent	....	....

I predict — you can't wait to do the experiment...

So you think you know what's going to happen, eh?... Well, in the next few pages you'll
get the chance to test it out and see if you're right. What are you waiting for...

Shadows of Different Materials

You need to do an experiment to test your predictions about the shadows of opaque, transparent and translucent materials...

Q1 (Circle) the things you should use to do the experiment.

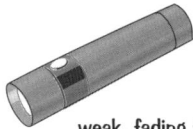

weak, fading torch

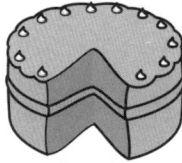

a big cake

big, strong torch

white paper or cardboard to look at the shadow on

collection of translucent, transparent and opaque objects

Somehow mealtime was less fun for Trevor's shadow.

Q2 Choose the correct sentence from each pair and write it on the notepad to make a complete set of instructions for the experiment.

Get 1 opaque, 1 transparent and 1 translucent material.*

Get 3 opaque materials and no others.

Put all the objects on different coloured tables.

Hold the objects over a piece of white cardboard.

Shine the same torch on each of the samples.

Shine a torch on one, a lamp on one and a candle on the other.

Sketch and write down what the shadows look like.

Record the sizes of the different things.

....
....
....
....
....
....
....

* See what your teacher has that you can use. Things which work well are: opaque - wood or foil; transparent - glass or acetate; translucent - nylon or gauze.

I really, really want to see those shadows...

If you change the torches and backgrounds, the shadows are bound to look different. Only change the materials — so you can see what difference the type of material makes.

Shadows of Different Materials

At last, after all that planning,
you can actually do the experiment...

Q1 Follow the instructions from Q2 on the last page. Draw in what you can see and write a description of the shadows.

Hint — Think about the colour and the darkness of the shadows.

OPAQUE material

Draw the object and its shadow:

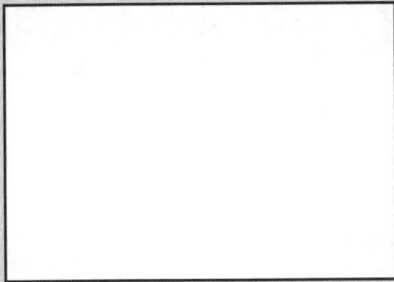

The shadow is...

....

....

TRANSPARENT material

Draw the object and its shadow:

The shadow is...

....

....

TRANSLUCENT material

Draw the object and its shadow:

The shadow is...

....

....

If you can't do the experiment, here are some sample answers to use: opaque object (eg. a book) - very dark shadow; transparent object (eg. window pane) - pale, faint shadow; translucent (eg. nylon tights) - not very dark shadow.

Q2 Write OPAQUE, TRANSLUCENT, or TRANSPARENT under the right description.

Darkest shadow: Medium shadow: Lightest shadow:

....

Shadow-tastic...

So, were your predictions right? We'll see on the next page...

Shadows of Different Materials

Now you've done the experiment you need to see what happened.
Then you can look back at your predictions to see if you were right.

Q1   This table is just like the one on page 19 where you wrote down what
you **thought** the shadows would be like. Fill in what **actually happened**.

Objects	They blocked out	The shadow was
Opaque	....	....
Transparent	....	....
Translucent	....	....

Q2   Choose the right words to finish off this conclusion.

light   different   darker   shadows

Shadows are made when an object blocks ....

Opaque, transparent and translucent objects

block .... amounts of light.

This means that their .... look different.

The more light an object blocks out,

the .... its shadow will be.

These shadows are everywhere...

Planning and doing these experiments can take quite a while. But they're good fun and
help you see what is happening — better than a boring book anyway.

Revision Questions

Here are lots of juicy questions to check that you know everything
in the world about light and shadows — well, almost.

Q1   What is the main source of light in the daytime?

....

Q2   Finish the sentence by putting a (ring) round the right word in the brackets.
Then put a tick by the correct picture of a shadow being made.

Shadows are made when objects

(BLOCK / MAKE) light.

Q3   Draw the shadows onto the pictures — but **only**
if there is definitely a shadow being made.

Terry's eyesight
was getting worse.

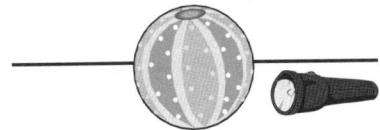

Q4   Draw lines to match each thing to its shadow.

We must keep in torch — I'll light a letter...

Some of these questions are spookily similar to questions on other pages.
So don't flap if you can't do them — just take a peek back over the book.

Revision Questions

Sorry — we haven't finished yet.
The end is in sight, but there are two more pages to go.

Q5 Write TRUE or FALSE next to the sentences below.

a) Shadows stay the same length during the day.

....

b) Shadows change length during the day.

....

Q6 Look at the picture of the Sun over the mountains at 9 am.
Put a tick (✓) by the right picture of the Sun at **4 pm**.

Q7 Finish the sentence by putting a (ring) round the right words in brackets.

The Sun does (THE SAME THING / DIFFERENT THINGS) every day.

Q8 Draw the Sun and an arrow to show where the light is going in the pictures below.

Q9 Look at the picture of the shadow stick. Then answer the questions.

a) Which shadow was measured at midday?

....

b) Was the Sun HIGH or LOW in the sky at this time?

....

No more fumbling in the dark...

Some of these questions might seem a bit tricky. But if you look back over previous pages you'll see that you can do them — no problem.

© CGP 2003

Revision Questions

OK, I give in. It's the final page. After this there are no more questions
to tax your brains. I bet you'll miss them when they're gone.

Q10 Finish the sentences by choosing the right words from the box.

The Earth .... round once each day.

This makes the .... seem to move through the sky.

But the Sun actually stays ....

> still   Earth
> spins   Sun

Q11 Give two examples of when you CAN'T use a sundial to tell the time.

① ....

② ....

Q12 Fill in the blanks to finish the table.

TYPE OF MATERIAL	AMOUNT OF LIGHT LET THROUGH	EXAMPLE
OPAQUE	Lets no light through	
	Lets some light through	Nylon tights
TRANSPARENT		Milk bottle

Q13 Draw lines to match each material to the colour of its shadow.

Tights

Glass

Wooden table

...these pages will make you brighter...

This is a sad moment — no more questions. Not one. Ahhh, go on then — just for you.
As I was going to St. Ives I met a man with seven wives. Each wife had seven sacks.
Each sack had seven cats. Each cat had seven kittens. How many were going to St. Ives?*

* One (just me. The rest were all going the other way.)

Index